NEVER
A STOCK
ON WEDNESDAY

NEVER SHORT A STOCK ON WEDNESDAY

*And 300 More Financial Lessons
You Can't Afford Not to Know*

NANCY DUNNAN

A HarperResource Book
from HarperPerennial

HarperCollins books may be purchased for educational, business, or sales promotional use. For information, please write to: Special Markets Department, HarperCollins Publishers Inc., 10 East 53rd Street, New York, New York 10022.

FIRST EDITION

Produced by Empire State Book Packagers

Library of Congress Cataloging-in-Publication Data is available upon request.

99 00 01 02 03❖/RRD 10 9 8 7 6 5 4 3 2 1

I've been rich, and I've been poor,
and believe me, rich is better.

SOPHIE TUCKER
1884–1966

ACKNOWLEDGMENTS

The author would like to thank these very special people who contributed their wit, wisdom, and time to this project:

Robert Wilson, my editor at HarperCollins, who conceived and fashioned this series.

Jay Pack, who added to and improved each entry.

Tim Hays, agent and designer for the book.

INTRODUCTION

SOPHIE TUCKER, the legendary American entertainer who died in 1966, was exactly right when she said being rich is a whole lot better than being poor. That advice is just as viable today as it was back then.

As we enter the twenty-first century, making smart decisions about saving, investing and spending money are as important as ever. In many instances, the decision making process will become more complicated—not only because we face a proliferation of financial options but because we must pay for increasingly expensive housing, education, longer lives and therefore greater medical and retirement needs.

I wrote this book to help you prepare for these dramatic changes, most notably the explosive growth of online trading, banking, saving and spending. Trips to your local bank, shopping center, broker's office and travel agent will decrease dramatically while purchasing, investing research via your computer will increase phenomenally. Twenty–four–hour trading will grow, and with it Internet scams. It goes without saying that the more you know, the smarter your decisions will be.

Sophie Tucker was diversified, starring on Broadway and in vaudeville, cabaret, burlesque, film and TV. She recorded her famous signature song, "Some of These Days," for the primitive Edison company in 1911, yet was also part of the Rock era.

She moved with the times. So must you.

Each lesson in this book will enable you to incorporate Sophie Tucker's wisdom. Read one lesson per day and by this time next year you will indeed be richer than you are today. Then, pass this book onto a friend and take joy in making that person richer as well.

Nancy Dunnan
New York City

"Anyone Can Hold the Helm
When the Sea Is Calm."

SAID BY THE ROMAN Pubilius Syrus in the first century B.C., this applies equally to the 21st century A.D. It's not too difficult to make money when the market is holding steady. The trick is riding out the choppy waters.

— ¢ —

Put Funds with High Portfolio Turnover Rates in Your 401(k).

MUTUAL FUNDS THAT continually buy and sell stocks generate capital gains taxes. But, you can shelter these taxes in 401(k) and other tax-deferred retirement accounts.

Never Buy a Mutual Fund in December.

THIS IS WHEN most funds pay shareholders their interest and dividends for the entire calendar year. If you own shares on the payout date, you'll owe taxes for the previous year—even if you bought shares just a day before distribution. **$TIP:** Call the fund and ask for the distribution date. Buy shares afterwards so you won't wind up paying someone else's tax bill.

Verify Those Online Trades.

IF YOU THINK your trade wasn't executed quickly or at the best price (and many are not) ask your brokerage firm for the "time stamp," a paper showing when your order was received and filled. A new ruling from the National Association of Security Dealers (NASD) requires every broker, including those online, to provide this information. **$TIP:** If you don't get results, click on: www.nasd.com or call NASD at: (301) 590–6500 and register your complaint. You'll get a written response.

Put Index Funds in Your Taxable Account.

BECAUSE THEY reflect the index they mirror, such as the S&P 500, there is very little buying and selling involved in this type of fund. That means you won't have to pay as much in capital gains tax as you would with a traditional stock fund.

Climb the Ladder With Your Bank CDs.

WHEN INTEREST RATES start to rise, divide your money among several CDs that have differing maturity dates. As rates move up you can take money from the shortest–term CD and reinvest it in a longer–term CD with a higher rate. This is known as "laddering."

Ignore Horse Whispers.

THESE UNPUBLISHED and unofficial "whisper estimates" of company earnings appear on cable TV shows and throughout the Internet before the official release of actual earnings. Whisper estimates, often higher than the final figures, typically originate with hedge fund managers and major stock traders. Leave them there.

Buy CDs Through Stockbrokers.

BECAUSE THEY SHOP the nation for the best deals, brokers often can offer one–half a percentage point or more than banks on FDIC–insured certificates. If you have a brokerage account, there should be no commission, no paperwork, no trouble other than a phone call.

Make Friends with Roth.

ONCE YOUR MONEY has been in a Roth IRA for five years, you can withdraw your contributions and earnings tax–free, as long as you're over age 59 $\frac{1}{2}$. And, if you don't wish to, you don't have to withdraw money—ever—whereas with a traditional IRA, you absolutely must start taking out money at age 70 $\frac{1}{2}$ and then those withdrawals are taxed.

Eyeball I-Bonds When Interest Rates Rise.

THE 30-YEAR U.S. Treasury I-Bond is indexed for inflation and its interest rate is adjusted periodically so you can take advantage of rising rates. Avoid fees by purchasing through the Treasury Direct program.

INFO: (800) 943–6864 or www.publicdebt.treas.gov

Don't Be Click-Happy.

A UNIVERSITY OF California-Davis study found that people who gave up trading by phone with a traditional stockbroker to trade online, traded more frequently, more speculatively, and less thoughtfully. **BOTTOM LINE:** They underperformed those who traded less often with a live broker. Avoid impulsivity.

Take Hold of Low Term–Insurance Rates.

COMPETITION AND longer life spans have driven down premiums to historic lows. Lock in low rates or convert your current policy to one with a longer term.

INFO: To find out how much coverage you need and to get comparative quotes, get in touch with Intelliquote Insurance Services, (888) 622–0925 or www.intelliquote.com

Be a Nine–to–Four Investor.

BROKERAGE FIRMS are starting to extend trading hours beyond the official 4 p.m. close of the market. Because trading is thin after–hours, volatility is high, and stock prices jump around for no apparent reason. If you insist on participating, put in limit orders, specifying the highest price at which you will buy and the lowest price at which you will sell.

Call Your Old Alma Mater.

IF YOU NEED CASH to launch a business, check with your Business School. Many help alums with venture capital. Among them: Columbia University, New York University's Stern School of Business, Northwestern University's Kellogg School of Management, the Anderson School at UCLA and (hopefully) yours.

Know the Big Four.

THE FOUR CRITERIA experts use for picking a winning growth stock are: 1) It's in a growing industry; 2) It's gaining industry share; 3) It has a strong balance sheet; and 4) It has an improving return on equity.

Go to the Dogs.

THE "DOGS OF THE DOW" theory has consistently generated above-average dividends and capital gains. Simply buy equal amounts of the ten highest-yielding stocks in the Dow Jones Industrial Average. Hold them one year, recalculate the list, sell stocks no longer on the top-ten list and replace them with those that are. **$TIP:** Get the list: www.dogsofthedow.com. Or, buy the Schwab Ten Trust, an equity-unit investment trust built around the ten stocks in the Dow with the highest dividend yields.

Instant Credit Reports.

NEED YOUR REPORT in a hurry? For $8, Experian, the largest of the credit bureaus, will deliver your report immediately. Click on: www.icreditreport.com. **$TIP:** If you've been refused credit, you're entitled to a free copy. Call any of the big three credit reporting bureaus directly: Experian: (800) 682–7654; Equifax: (800) 685–1111; TransUnion: (800) 888–4213

Opt for Options.

IF YOU'VE NEVER traded options or are rusty, get up to speed by practicing with simulated trades using "The Toolbox," a primer put together by the Chicago Board of Options Exchange at: www.cboe.com. Click on "Education."

INFO: Two option–friendly online brokers: Tradeoptions: www.tradeoptions.com, and Discover Brokerage Direct: www.lombard.com

Know What Your Savings Bonds Are Worth.

BANKS AREN'T much help in this area anymore. In fact, it isn't easy to find a live teller. Instead, download "Savings Bond Wizard" from the Bureau of Public Debt. You can find this at www.savingsbonds.gov. It's free. Your bond values will be updated biannually and those that have stopped earning interest are flagged.

— ¢ —

Less Is More.

Mies Van der Rohe was right—too much detail gets in the way. Owning too many mutual funds leads to overlapping investments and overloading on paperwork. **SOLUTION:** Sell shares in funds that have similar holdings but keep the one that's been the best performer for the last three to five years. (Impress your friends: Van der Rohe's first name was Ludwig.)

— ¢ —

Head for Small Claims Court.

TAX DISPUTES involving as much as $50,000 (not including interest) can now be heard in the Small Case Division of the Tax Court. The filing fee is $60 and you don't need a lawyer. **INFO:** Clerk of the Court, U.S. Tax Court, 400 Second Street NW, Washington, DC 20217; call: (202) 606–8754.

Buy Snow Shovels in June.

BOATS IN JANUARY. Air conditioners in February. Winter coats in April. Skis in May. Wool sweaters in June. Snow blowers in July. Barbecues in October. Bikinis in December. You get the idea.

Do's for Day Traders.

OR FREQUENT TRADERS. Never risk more than 5% of your capital on any one trade. And always set a stop–loss order, telling your online broker to automatically sell a stock when its price drops a certain percentage below what you paid for it.

Reverse Your Real Estate Thinking.

IF YOU'RE AT LEAST 62 and not worried about leaving your home to heirs, you can get money from it with a reverse mortgage. **$TIP:** For approved lenders, call Fannie Mae: (800) 732–6643

Take a Rain Check.

WHEN STORES have special sales, or two–for–one deals, hot items are gone long before the sale is over. Most supermarkets will give you a rain check to use when they restock. **$TIP:** Always ask: the manager isn't in the aisles voluntarily passing them out.

Money Is Not Necessary for Making Money.

DON'T PUT OFF investing because you don't have a huge stash of cash. Time—not the dollars involved—is the critical element because compound interest works with any amount, large or small. Start now, whether it's $10, $100, $1,000, $10,000 or $100,000.

— ¢ —

Keep Awake.

THE BEST TIME to make airline reservations is between midnight and 1 A.M. That's when airlines load low-priced airfares into computers and restore bargain seats that were booked but not ticketed.

Don't Lose Track of Your Children.

YOU NOW CAN CLAIM a $400 tax credit on your 1040 for each qualifying child under 17. Qualifying means a child you claim as an exemption and who is your child, stepchild or eligible foster child. If your AGI is under $110,000 (married) or $75,000 (single), claim this credit on line 43.

Follow the Leader.

BUY STOCK IN a company when its executives are buying and sell when they're selling.

INFO: "Insider Chronicle" reports on those who file Form 4 with the SEC; that includes people who own 10% of a company or who are decision-makers for the firm. Call (800) 243-2324 or click on: www.cda.com/insidernet

Take Your Money & Run.

SECTION 72(T) of the IRS code allows distributions before age 59 1/2 from IRAs, without a 10% early withdrawal penalty, if you follow these rules: 1) You must take payments at least annually; 2) Payments must be taken for at least five years or until you reach 59 1/2 (whichever is later); 3) Distributions must remain virtually equal.

INFO: For a free copy of "Using Your IRAs for Early Retirement," call: (877) 368–1470.

Help the Bride & Groom Put a Roof Over Their Heads.

ADVISE THEM to open a Bridal Registry Account with a participating FHA bank or lender. Then family and friends can deposit cash gifts directly into an account held in the couple's names.

INFO: www.hud.gov/bridal.html

— ¢ —

Split for Splits.

PURCHASE STOCKS that are likely to split within twelve months. Companies that declare stock splits usually outperform the overall market for twelve to eighteen months after the split. Stocks likely to split trade at $85 or higher, and have a history of rising dividends.

Walk, Don't Run, to Your Mutual Fund.

IF YOU HEAR a fund is about to close to new investors, don't assume it's hot. Ten of fifteen equity funds that closed the gates last year underperformed their peers for the rest of the year.

Think Insurance First, Car Second.

INSURANCE RATES vary widely. Get rates for several cars from several insurance companies, then decide. Most costly to insure: BMW, Mitsubishi, Porsche, Toyota, Acura, Mercedes. Least costly: Chevrolet, Mercury, Oldsmobile, Saturn, Buick.

Pay Only for What You Use.

IF ALL YOU DO at your healthclub is run on a treadmill and climb steps, you don't need to pay dues for a gym that has a swimming pool, sauna, hot tub, tennis courts and seaweed wraps.

Neither Shrink nor Insure the Kids.

ALTHOUGH PREMIUMS are inexpensive, put those dollars toward your life insurance or the kids' college education. Life insurance is to protect those who depend upon the insured for support. Children depend upon their parents, not vice–versa.

Invest in Aging.

OVER THE NEXT 15 years, the number of Americans who will live to more than 85 will grow dramatically. Pick companies involved in the graying of America such as: Healthcare Services Group, Health & Retirement Properties, General Nutrition, Express Scripts, Lincare Holdings.

Have Your Cake & Eat It Too with Convertible Preferreds.

THEY COMBINE income and growth: the dividend on a company's preferred stock is considerably higher than it is on the common and yet the preferred can be converted into the common when it's to your advantage. BOTTOM LINE: with preferreds, you earn income during turbulent markets by collecting dividends and then again if the stock rises in price and you sell.

Boggle the Experts By Following Bogle.

JOHN BOGLE, who founded the Vanguard Group 25 years ago, advises picking an actively–managed stock fund that: 1) Has an annual expense ratio of 0.75% per year or less; and 2) Has an annual portfolio turnover of less than 40%.

Discover Your Fund's True Cost.

THIS HAS NEVER been easy, but the SEC's new Mutual Fund Cost Calculator does the job. After you plug in fees, expense ratios, anticipated return and holding period, you'll find out how much it costs to own the fund.

INFO: www.sec.gov

Stick With Your Day Job.

A MAJORITY OF day traders are into the red within six months to a year, often because they buy and sell nonstop, totting up huge costs—the average day trader's annual expenses (commissions plus the cost of margin loans) are over 50%. That means in order to break even they must make a 50% profit. It's a whole lot easier and less stressful to simply collect a paycheck! Trade at a reasonable pace.

Invest with the Teenies.

THE NEXT GENERATION TRUST, a Morgan Stanley Dean Witter fund, invests in companies that cater to teenagers with money to spend. You can do the same—purchase stocks of companies that sell clothing, computer games and entertainment that appeal to kids. Or get the prospectus: (800) 869–6397.

Prefer Preferreds.

IF YOU WANT to minimize risk. Dividends on preferred stocks are fixed and paid to stockholders before dividends are distributed to those owning common shares—a good position to be in if the company is having a tough year.

Check Out a Charity First.
Donate Second.

THERE ARE THOUSANDS of scams in the arena of doing good. To find out if a charity is legit and donations to it are tax-exempt, simply click on www.irs.ustreas.gov for an IRS-approved list of organizations.

Make Good Mistakes.

THE ONLY "BAD" mistake is one from which you never learn. View investment mistakes as lessons rather than failures. Write down what went wrong and why.

Buy Stocks with Rising Dividends if You're a Buy–and–Hold Investor.

THEY TEND TO hold up better during market declines and the dividends themselves help offset the sting of declining prices.

Use Two Pockets to Foil One Pickpocket.

PUT CASH IN ONE pocket, traveler's checks in another and credit cards and passport in separate places. Even the nimblest of thieves has trouble stealing from more than one spot on one person at one time.

Get a Home Energy Checkup.

BELIEVE IT OR NOT, some turned–off appliances use power. Find out how to save as much as 100% on your annual energy bill with the Alliance To Save Energy, a non–profit group.
INFO: www.ase.org

High–Five the High Dividend Stocks.

PICK THOSE that have raised their dividends every year for at least five years. **TOP FIVE:** Central & Southwest, Crescent Real Estate, Duke Energy, Equity Residential REIT and RJR Nabisco.

Protect Your Medicare Rights.

ONGOING CUTS IN benefits, increasing premiums and other negatives should put you on alert. For an explanation of your rights, call: (800) MEDICARE or click on: www.medicare.gov.

— ¢ —

Go for Two.

OPEN TWO ONLINE brokerage accounts. When online outages or excessive volume blocks access to one, use the other.

Buy Euro–Denominated Traveler's Checks.

YOU'LL AVOID CURRENCY exchange fees (2% to 5%) in these countries: Austria, Belgium, Finland, France, Germany, Ireland, Italy, Luxembourg, the Netherlands, Portugal and Spain. **$TIP:** Call American Express: (800) 221–7292 or Thomas Cook: (800) 223–4030.

Don't Get Shagged.

A GROWING NUMBER of credit card issuers don't consider payments as being on time unless they arrive by 10 a.m. the day they're due.

— ¢ —

Stay Put. At Least Two Years.

WHEN YOU SELL A primary residence where you've lived at least two years, up to $500,000 of your capital gain is tax free if you file a joint return; it's $250,000 on a single return.

Get the Most Bang for Your Banking Buck.

SHOP THE INTERNET to find: no-fee ATMs, top rates on checking and saving accounts and low rates on loans. **THREE BEST SITES:** Banksite—www.banksite.com; Bank Rate Monitor—www.bankrate; Surcharge—www.surcharge-free-atms.com.

Keep Clicking Until You Find the Best.

FOR CONTINUALLY updated rankings of online brokerage firms, based on their speed, accuracy, dependability, research and extra services, use:

Gomez Advisors: www.gomez.com

Expert Online: www.xolia.com

Keynote Systems: www.keynote.com

Come on to Commodity Stocks.

WHEN INFLATION RISES, prices of commodities follow suit. Look at stocks of oil, timber, mining, metal and agricultural companies. The more inflation rises, the better commodoties are likely to perform.

Moves for Nervous Nellies.

IF YOU'RE ANXIOUS about the future yet feel you're missing out on the bull market, invest 40% in solid blue chip stocks or stock mutual funds and divide the rest between Treasuries and money market funds. That way, you'll sleep through the night.

Shop Duty–Free.

WHEN TRAVELING ABROAD, look for antiques more than 100 years old, cut diamonds that are not set, original works of art, and unstrung pearls. They're all duty free. Skip: fruits, vegetables, meat, poultry and drugs. With the first four you'll be hit with a customs duty fee; with the last, a jail sentence.

Cash in on IRS Giveaways.

THE IRS HAS MORE than $68 million in unclaimed tax refund checks that were sent out but returned because of delivery problems. The average amount is $690. **$TIP:** To find out if you're one of these lucky people, call: (800) 829–1040.

Know Your Fund's Turnover Rate.

IT'S GIVEN IN THE prospectus. A rate of 100% means the fund holds its portfolio positions, on average, for one year. A 50% rate means two years. Put a fund with high turnover rate in a tax-sheltered account to shelter the capital gains tax the fund generates as the manager turns over the portfolio.

Be Patient.

WAIT FOR THE perfect time to buy stocks: in a slow market, or when a temporary setback has pushed a smart company's shares down in price.

Take a Dip.

TO SPOT ENGINE trouble in a used car, check the dipstick. Lots of gunk at the end generally indicates a bad thermostat or a blown seal. Pick another car.

Introduce Your Kids to Roth.

NOT PHILIP, but the Roth IRA. As soon as your child has earned income, open one. Then be a sport: let him save his earned income and fund the Roth with money received as a gift—from you, his grandparents, others. This gives him a chance to double-up savings or maybe spend some of his summer earnings on pizza, baseball caps and music CDs.

Don't Toss Out Old Appliances.

PARTS FOR MANY, regardless of the company or manufacturer, are available through Sears Part–Direct: (800) 469–4663.

–¢–

Turn Your Bonus into Tax–Free Income.

DITTO FOR A RAISE. Find out if you can put this "found" money in your company's 401(k) or other retirement plan. And ask if it also qualifies for an employer–matching contribution.

Never Bury Your Head in the Sand.

INSTEAD, FIND OUT how much money you need to save for retirement. **$TIP:** Get the Retirement Planning Worksheet, from T. Rowe Price: (800) 225–5132 or www.troweprice.com; and The Ballpark Estimator: www.asce.org.

Invest in Diamonds.

THIS STOCK, found on the NYSE under the symbol DIA, represents the 30 stocks that make up the Dow Jones Industrial Average. Similar to an index mutual fund, it has no minimum investment requirement and shares trade throughout the day, so you can buy or sell any time. (Most index funds, in contrast, come with a $2,500 minimum and their price isn't determined until the end of the day.)

Play Two Top Ten Lists.

THE PAYDEN–Rygel Growth and Income Fund keeps half its assets in the top–ten yielding Dow Jones Industrial Average stocks, and half in the S&P 500.

INFO: (800) 572–9336

— ¢ —

Buy in an Inexpensive Fund Family.

THOSE THAT HAVE the lowest costs are: TIAA-CREF; T. Rowe Price; USAA; Vanguard Group

Make a Tax–Free Gift.

YOU CAN GIVE any dollar amount free of gift tax to pay someone else's medical or tuition bills—provided you pay the billing institution directly.

Wait to Resign from Your Job.

CHECK FIRST TO SEE if you're fully vested in the company's retirement plan. Full vesting, when the money is yours to keep, may take five or seven years. If you're close, hang tough.

Buy Favorites when They're Out of Favor.

MAKE A LIST OF household names and buy on dips. Solid blue–chip companies eventually recover; when they do, you'll reap a profit. Remember—even IBM once tanked, hitting a low around $12, before Big Blue made a remarkable recovery.

What You See Is What You Get.

IF YOU'RE SELLING a house that needs repairs, list it as a "handy-man's special" or an "as is" property. Put it in writing so the buyer knows what he sees is what he gets. To help close the deal, offer to get estimates from several reliable contractors.

Dine by Candlelight.

YOUR ELECTRIC LIGHTS account for up to 13% of your bill.

Name a Beneficiary of Your 401(k).

IF YOU DON'T, most plans make your estate the beneficiary, which delays payment to heirs, triggers other taxes, adds probate expenses. $TIP: If you're married, federal law requires your spouse receive your entire 401(k), even if you've named another beneficiary. Exception: If your spouse gives written consent for you to name another beneficiary.

Donate Your Old Clunker.

THE NATIONAL Kidney Foundation will pick up any car, running or not, almost anywhere. Keep a duplicate of the Foundation's estimate of the car's value—for your records and for the IRS, which requires written records of charitable gifts exceeding $250. **$TIP:** If the donation is over $500, attach Form 8283, "Noncash Charitable Contributions," to your 1040. If the amount is $5,000, you'll need a written appraisal; the appraiser must sign Part II in Section B of Form 8283.

INFO: National Kidney Foundation: (800) 488–2277.

Bear–Proof Your Portfolio.

WHEN YOU THINK the market is too high, take gains by selling the portion of a stock or mutual fund that represents your original cost. This way you not only take a profit but you still hold a position, just a smaller one. Put the proceeds in bonds, growth and income funds or Treasuries.

Buy Small.

TO BE MORTGAGE–free at an early age, purchase a house that you can afford with a 15–year rather than a 30–year mortgage. Then, starting in the sixteenth year, take the money that you were using to pay down your mortgage and 1) Fund your children's college education; 2) Add to your retirement nest–egg; 3) Go on a toot.

Be Nice & Queue Up.

IT MAY PAY OFF. Add shares of QQQ, which trades on the AMEX, to your portfolio. Because this stock replicates the NASDAQ 100 Index, it's a no–brainer way to play Internet and communication stocks. And, use it as a market indicator. In other words, don't short if the price is holding firm. This indicates that the market will soon rise.

Don't Forget Nice Ginnie Mae.

THESE GOVERNMENT National Mortgage Association securities (GNMAs) consist of pools of FHA and VA mortgages. Guaranteed by the U.S. government, yields tend to be ½ to 2½ percent higher than on long–term Treasury bonds. Don't have the minimum $25,000? Invest through a GNMA mutual fund.

Go Bi.
Bi–Weekly, that Is.

YOU'LL REDUCE the life of your 30–year mortgage, depending on your interest rate, anywhere from 11 to 18 years. Simply divide your monthly mortgage payments in half and pay the mortgage every two weeks instead of monthly. You'll wind up making an extra month's payment every year.

Never Say You're Sorry.

IF YOU HAVE A fender bender, keep quiet. Anything that sounds like you're admitting responsibility could be used against you later on. Give out only your name, address and car registration and only to the other driver, to anyone injured and to the police. Before leaving the scene, get the names and phone numbers of any witnesses.

Pay Close Attention to Corporate Buy–Backs.

WHEN A COMPANY buys back its own stock, management thinks it's cheap. So should you. Regard this as a buying opportunity.

Big Is Better.

STOCKS OF COMPANIES whose CEOs are paid above–average salaries (and who have business savvy) tend to outperform the market. Track salaries in *Forbes, Fortune,* and the *Wall Street Journal.*

Parent Tuition Alert: Pay off Credit Card Balances.

DO SO BEFORE applying for financial aid. Although colleges don't take credit card debt into account when determining aid–eligibility, they do count money in the bank and expect a percentage of it to be used for college costs. Instead, use that money to reduce both your debt and your net assets and thus boost the likelihood you'll receive financial help. **$TIP:** For a gold mine of information, click on: www.finaid.org.

Know Your Mutual Fund's Fax Number.

AND ITS LOCAL, direct phone number. Then, if you need to buy or sell shares in a hurry and the toll–free number is busy or you can't reach a live person, you have two alternatives. **$TIP:** Also find out if your fund has a walk–in office nearby.

Sell When You've Made a Mistake.

DETERMINE A percentage, say 10%, and get out when your stock has dropped that much from the original price.

Health Is Wealth.

EXERCISE, DRINK lots of water, take vitamins, stop smoking and drink in moderation. You'll cut your health insurance premiums and be able to enjoy the money you made by following the lessons in this book.

Sell When You've Made a Profit.

DETERMINE A percentage, say 30%, and get out when the stock has gone up that much from the price you paid. If you think it's still on a roll, sell 50% of your position.

Know the IRS's Favorite Red Flags.

FOUR ITEMS THAT ARE likely to trigger an audit: Underreported income, especially if you have an expensive lifestyle (the worst possible red flag); high business expenses and a low gross–profit margin; lots of meal deductions; hobby losses claimed as business expenses. Never underreport income, if only a few hundred or thousand dollars.

Never Pay Full Rate for a Rental Car.

ASK FOR A DISCOUNT if you're a member of AARP, AAA, automobile clubs, frequent flyer programs, just about anything. And look for promos through Guide to Rental Cars at: www.bnm.com and Car Rental Direct at: www.carrental-direct.com.

Get Tax-Free Income.

RENT OUT your home, or a vacation home, for no more than 14 days a year and the rental income you pocket is 100% tax free.

— ¢ —

Click Your Mouse.

GO TO: www.ftmanagement.com/tradingonline. This site has links to some of the best online brokers, making it an easy way to compare services, account requirements and fees.

Lower Your Student Loan Rates.

SOME LENDERS cut the interest rate if you sign up for automatic deductions from your checking or savings account. Other strategies: make all payments on time and get the interest rate cut by 2%; and find out if your interest is tax deductible—it may be if your income is below a certain level.

Turn Losses into Winners.

KEEP A RECORD of all the money you lose gambling—at the casino, the race track, church raffle, bingo parlor or your state lottery. Losses can be offset against winnings to shelter them from taxes. **$TIP:** Although winnings over $600 are reported to the IRS, it's up to you to document your losses. And you may never deduct more than you have won.

Don't Take Any Wooden Pennies.

PENNY STOCKS, that is. These speculative equities seem appealing because they trade for under $5. Yet, they can't be listed on the New York or American exchanges because they don't meet the exchanges' capital requirements. And, many are issued by companies with very short or erratic earnings, or both. Leave them to those who have millions of pennies they can afford to lose.

Put Your Savings Bonds on Autopilot.

THE TREASURY Department's new Easysaver Plan lets you purchase both EE and I (inflation–indexed) bonds through automatic monthly transfers from your savings or checking account. The bonds are then mailed to you. The interest earned escapes state and local taxes and you can put off paying federal income tax until you cash in your bonds or they stop earning interest (in 30 years).
INFO: (877) 811–7283 or: www.easysaver.gov

Shop for a House in the Rain.

SELLERS TEND to be willing to accept less than the offering price because in dreary weather they know their house looks dreary.

$$-\cent-$$

Faint Heart Never Won
Fair Maid—or Man.

DO YOUR HOMEWORK before investing. Then, having done it, have the courage of your convictions.

Trust Your Broker.

IF A BROKER HOLDS your stock certificates: You don't have to worry about them being lost or stolen. You can have a margin account. You can place limit orders more easily. You can meet the three–day deadline to turn over shares to your broker when you sell, and without having to pay an overnight courier to get them there in time. **$TIP:** Ask if your broker charges an inactivity fee if you don't trade regularly.

Never Be Fully Margined.

BORROW LESS than 50% so you can weather temporary price declines. And check the closing prices of margined stocks twice a week.

— ¢ —

Use Stop Orders.

TELL YOUR BROKER to automatically sell your margined stocks if they fall below a stated price. You'll avoid an even larger loss if you've margined a stock that's tanking.

Keep Your Driver's License Close to Your Chest.

DON'T LET A CAR dealer or anyone else make a copy. It could be used to get your credit report, determine what type of risk you are, find out if you've been late on payments—all things that hamper a good financing offer.

Nine Companies with Zero Debt.

1) BOB EVANS FARMS 2) Dollar General 3) Dun & Bradstreet 4) A.G. Edwards 5) Family Dollar Stores 6) Walgreen Co. 7) Washington Post Co. 8) Weis Markets 9) Wrigley

Jump–Start Your Retirement Savings.

TO GET GOING, use this rule of thumb: subtract your age from 100. That's the suggested percentage you should be investing in stocks. Use it only as a benchmark.

Emotion Is Your Enemy.

THOUGHTFUL DECISIONS, steady saving and clear–headed invest-ing always win out over erratic research, impulsive moves, and over the top thinking.

— ¢ —

Time Is Your Friend.

OVER THE LONG–TERM, stocks outperform other types of invest-ments, including bonds, Treasuries and money market funds. So, resist jumping in and out of the market.

Dribble Forward.

IF YOU WANT TO raise a specific amount of cash by a particular date, resist selling all your fund shares at once. Instead, use dollar cost averaging on the sell side by selling the same dollar amount every quarter or every month. You'll lock in profits even when the fund's performance is down.

If You Can't Eat It, Leave It

SUPERMARKETS AND convenience stores seldom have great prices on non–food products: kitchen jimjiks, shampoo, aspirin, furniture polish. Compare prices with Wal–Mart, Sam's, Kmart and discount drugstores. By shopping for the right products at the right place you'll save up to 60%.

Skip the Three "T"s.

TIPSTERS, TELEPHONE solicitations and TV hype. Instead, do your own research, ask your broker for his, write down three reasons for buying a particular stock, bond or mutual fund and sleep on it. Review your rationale the next day. If in the cold light of the morning it still seems solid, follow through.

Insure Your Stock Position.

SELL A CALL AT a higher price and buy a put at a lower one. The put will limit your loss.

Never Go House Hunting Without a Pre–Approved Mortgage.

THIS INVOLVES submitting a loan application in return for a lender's commitment that you can borrow up to a set dollar amount. Pre–approval enables you to move quickly when you spot a bargain.

Remember to Get Permission.

IF YOU'RE PLANNING a yard sale, find out if you need a legal permit. Although many municipalities insist upon them, they don't advertise the fact. Yet, ignore the law and you'll be fined—perhaps as much as you make in the sale. And, check your homeowner's insurance to see if it covers anyone who gets hurt on your property. If not, get a floater or umbrella policy.

Order Annual Reports for Free.

IF YOU DON'T know where a company is headquartered you can get its annual report from Investor Communications Business, which has reports from 3,500 U.S., U.K. and Canadian companies.

INFO: (800) 965–2929 (24 hours/day) or: www.icbinc.com

Head for Cover.

SELLING COVERED calls on your stocks will increase your income. If the stock price is stable, you keep the proceeds of the call. But if your stock is called away (goes up), you make a profit.

— ¢ —

Never Put All Your College Investments in a Custodial Account.

MONEY SAVED IN your child's name becomes his or hers on turning 18 or 21, depending upon the state. That means he can spend it as he likes—on college, on a car, on club life.

Get Ready for College.

IF YOU BEGIN investing $94 a month at 10%, starting when your child is one year old, you'll have a college fund of close to $50,000 by the time freshman year rolls around.

Invest in the Future.

SPOT TRENDS, such as outsourcing. With more firms hiring independent contractors or temporary employees, stocks including Automatic Data Processing, On Assignment Inc., Robert Half International and Korn Ferry should outperform the market.

Put Your Mutual Fund
to the Test.

COMPARE ITS PERFORMANCE with that of a major market index, such as the S&P 500. Keep only those stock funds that consistently beat the market by 2%, with the exception of index funds, which of course, simply mirror the index.

Know if You Need Wind Coverage.

SOME STATES HAVE started requiring those living in high risk areas to buy wind insurance. Call your state insurance department to find out if yours is one.

Think Before You Leap. Cut Back on Card-Jumping.

CHANGING YOUR credit card balance from one card to another may trigger a new 2% to 4% fee per transfer. Read the fine print first before you jump. It may pay to stay put.

Go for the Odd–Balls.

RATES ON ODD–TERM bank CDs tend to be higher than those on standard–length CDs. Because banks like to stagger maturities (so huge numbers of CDs won't be coming due at the same time) as an incentive, some offer better interest on the odd balls. Shop around and ask.

Trading Is Not Investing.

TRADING IS LIKE gambling. If your goal is long–term wealth, invest—don't trade.

—¢ —

Be Agent–Free.

WHEN SHOPPING for automobile insurance, consider a company that doesn't use agents. Rates will be lower. Amica Mutual: (800) 242–6422; Nationwide: (888) 634–7328

Put in for Puts.

IF YOU'RE NOT adverse to risk and think a stock will fall in price, buy puts. This strategy is safer than using a stop–loss order, which automatically triggers a "sell" if a stock drops to a certain price. A put is an option giving you the right (but not the obligation) to sell a stock at a predetermined price until a certain date. Puts are available on most stocks for a few dollars–per–100 shares. **$TIP:** Set your put options to sell if a stock rises 25% above the price you paid,or if it falls 5% to 10%.

Address Car Financing.

To FIND THE LOWEST interest rates from car dealers, check with www.carfinance.com.

Keep on Working.

EMPLOYERS LIKE older employees because they get to work on time, are polite, aren't into body–piercing, and appreciate the paycheck. **$TIP:** For help finding a job, consult Green Thumb, a national organization that provides training and employment for mature workers.

INFO: www.greenthumb.org.

Desperation Leads to Concessions.

BUY A HOUSE FROM an owner who is forced to sell. You'll get a much lower price if the seller has been transferred to another city, has already bought another piece of property or has died and the heirs don't wish to live there.

Don't Pay Off Your Mortgage Early.

AT LEAST NOT UNTIL you have an emergency nest–egg with three to six months worth of living expenses in it. Making extra payments ties up money in your house and if you are laid off or have serious financial problems, you don't want to be forced to sell the roof over your head.

Never Invite an IRS Auditor to Your House for Coffee.

YOU'D BE GIVING him an opportunity to scrutinize you, your surroundings, your lifestyle. Instead, have an accountant, enrolled agent or lawyer meet with the auditor at an office.

— ¢ —

Failing Up.

RUN STOCK PICKS by a friend or relative who lacks investment savvy. Buy those he doesn't like; skip over those he does.

Never Call Your Broker on Monday.

BUT WHEN HE CALLS, take notes. Tell him you'll think it over. And get back to him within a day. **$TIP:** For a free copy of a fill–in–the–blank form that helps you ask the right questions and record your broker's buy and sell recommendations, send a self–addressed, stamped, business–sized envelope to: Investors Take Note, North American Securities Administrators Association, 10 G Street NE, Washington, DC 20002.

Update Your Beneficiaries.

IF YOU HAVE MARRIED, been widowed, have a baby, have a grand-child, or get divorced, you may want to change who receives your IRA, 401(k) and any trusts you have.

Name Contingent–Beneficiaries.

YOU WANT TO AVOID having your money wind up in your estate—should your only beneficiary die. (When money falls into your estate, it triggers an immediate income–tax bill.)

Hire Your Kids and Deduct Their Salaries.

THE IRS REQUIRES that you pay them a reasonable wage for the type of work they do and document their hours. Earned income also means your children can open a ROTH IRA. **$TIP:** If you claim them as dependents, they can earn up to $4,300/year before federal taxes kick in.

Power–Surge Your Profits.

DEREGULATION IN the utility industry has led to new products, services and market share. Pick companies with an edge, such as Teco Energy, Duke Energy, New Century and Cinergy.

Be Ready When the Bubble Bursts.

IF YOU'RE HOLDING Internet or other hot stocks at incredibly high prices, reduce your exposure to 5% to 15% of your portfolio. You'll still profit from upswings but reduce severe losses if the mania ends.

Never Be Without Health Insurance.

IF YOU DON'T HAVE coverage because you work at home, the premiums are too high, or your employer doesn't offer it, it is possible to find affordable coverage. Start with: Netquote Insurance Shopper at: www.netquote.com. This free consumer service has a database of information on 5,000 insurance agents and 100 insurers. After answering a series of health and financial questions, you'll receive a recommendation for the cheapest plan given your situation, usually within a couple of days.

Close in on a Foreclosed Home.

THEY TEND TO BE less expensive than others in the same neighborhood but more likely to be in poor condition. Ask local real estate agents and lenders for possibilities.

INFO: Fannie Mae: www.fanniemae.com and Freddie Mac: www.freddiemac.com have huge databases. Search by city and price. (Freddie will even send you an e-mail when a house matching your description shows up.)

Move to the Woods.

LEADING COLLEGES prefer geographical diversity in a student body. Your child is more likely to get into a top school if he applies from a less competitive area or prep school.

Consider the Woods.

IF YOU FEEL YOUR family won't qualify for financial aid, look at smaller colleges in the south and midwest. Many offer scholarships to attract students from big cities and other parts of the country.

Freebies from Companies.

SHAREHOLDERS OFTEN receive perks from companies; check with the investor relations division of any company whose stock you own. Current goodies: • Discounts on Radio Shack products from Tandy Corp. • Gift packs of gum at Christmas from William Wrigley Jr., Co. • A 15% discount on theme park admissions and up to 25% off on catalog gift products from Anheuser–Busch. • Shareholders' rates at some hotels.

Spin the Wheel of Fortune.

SPIN–OFF COMPANIES (companies that were divisions of corporations and have recently gone public) on average, outperform the S&P 500 by ten percentage points per year during their first year of independence. **$TIP:** Standard & Poor's "The Outlook" lists potential and recent spin–offs on a regular basis.

Put Tax-Efficient Mutual Funds in Taxable Accounts.

THESE ARE STOCK funds that generate long–term gains (taxed at only 20%) or index funds that aren't actively managed and thus generate few or no taxable gains.

Buy Skis and Scuba Gear at Discount.

UNCLAIMED ITEMS and stuff we leave behind on airlines are sold via the Internet often at 80% below retail. Up to 200 items are listed at a time. Click on: www.unclaimedbaggage.com.

Talk to Yourself First,
Then Your Broker.

KNOW WHETHER you're investing for growth (price appreciation) or income. Make a list of industries or companies you know and like. Then, listen to your broker but in the end, let common sense and experience be your guide.

Find Out How Long Long-Term Insurance Really Is.

CRUNCH THE NUMBERS (or ask your accountant to do the work) in order to determine how long you would have to be in a nursing home to recoup your premiums. Then, skip any policy that would take more than one year, or requires a hospital stay before the benefits kick in and that doesn't specifically cover Alzheimer's disease.

Make Your Own Semi–Annual Report.

EVERY SIX MONTHS, send or e–mail your broker a summary of any changes in your financial life—a raise, bonus, new job, loss of job, marriage, birth of a child, divorce, a new address, purchase or sale of a house, etc. Not only does your broker need this information to make wise recommendations, it also lets him know you're keeping an eye on your portfolio and on him.

Treat an Investment Decision as You Would a Business Decision.

LINE UP THE FACTS. Study the situation. Have a fallback position. Then proceed.

Get Rid of Your PMI.

A NEW LAW REQUIRES automatic termination of Private Mortgage Insurance premiums when you've paid at least 20% of the home's value. (Lenders require PMI if you can't make a large enough down–payment.)

Don't Waste Money on Rent: Buy a House with Just 3% Down.

THE "FLEXIBLE 97" program from HUD allows people with good credit but little savings to purchase a house with a 3% downpayment. And, the 3% can come from your family, employer, a 401(k) loan or even from the seller.

INFO: Fannie Mae: (800) 7–FANNIE; www.fanniemae.com.

Diamonds Are a Girl's Best Friend.
And a Man's, Too.

"DIAMONDS" IS THE nickname for a stock through which you can trade the Dow Jones Industrial Average. It represents a basket of the 30 stocks that make up the Dow. Many mutual funds measure their performance by keeping up with the DJIA. Now you can buy it—the symbol is DIA.

Pay Now, Own Later. Use Warrants to Get in on the Action.

WARRANTS ARE OFFERED as sweeteners in the sale of a company's stock or bonds. You pay a small price for the right to buy a certain number of shares at a fixed price in the future. However, buy warrants only of a stock you would buy anyway.

Go from B–2–C to B–2–B.

THE FIRST WAVE of successful Internet stocks involved companies doing business directly with consumers, such as amazon.com and priceline.com. That was known as "B–2–C." The next wave will be businesses doing businesses with other businesses, or "B–2–B." Research ways to participate.

Shortcut Finding the Right Retirement Community.

WHETHER YOU'RE looking for yourself or for an aging relative, let someone else do the walking. Search by type of facility or by state with these two services: Retirement Living Information Center, (203) 938–0417 or www.retirementliving.com; Senior Resource: (858) 793–7714 or www.seniorresource.com.

Never Buy a Stock Without Knowing How Much Debt It's Carrying.

You know you shouldn't be too deep in debt: neither should a company. Check the debt–equity ratio, which shows how much debt there is compared with shareholders' equity (or book value). The lower the figure the better. Look for companies whose debt is no more than one–third of shareholders' equity.

Leave Wall Street Behind.

REGIONAL STOCKBROKERS throughout the country know and follow companies headquartered in their area, often discovering companies long before Wall Street—and before the price runs up. Open an account with at least one regional broker. You'll find them in Minneapolis, Milwaukee, Memphis and elsewhere.

Know Your Numbers.

TO TELL WHETHER a stock trades over–the–counter or through Nasdaq or on a stock exchange, count the number of letters in its symbol. Three letters or less indicates the New York or American exchanges. Four or more letters, it's a Nasdaq or OTC stock.

Don't Confuse Streaming with Snapping.

WHEN CHECKING A price of a single stock on the Web, you'll receive what's known as a snap quote. If you receive a continually updated flow of prices on your screen, you're getting streaming quotes. **CAUTION:** Streaming quotes are usually but not always in real-time. Know before you trade.

A Snare and a Delusion.

THE "PUMP & DUMP" ploy, a growing phenomenon on the Internet, occurs when a company or an individual publicizes unreasonably high profits and other hype to drive up a stock's price to new highs: that's the pumping part. These same people then sell their shares at the top: that's the dumping part. It's done through bulletin boards, chats, and e–mail messages as well as via phony research reports.

Uncheck the Checkmarks.

WHEN GETTING FINANCIAL information on the Web, look carefully to see if boxes on the form have already been checked. They typically give the site permission to e–mail you and often to share your e–mail with other sites. To prevent this, uncheck the box and then click 'SEND.'

Find Missing Pension Money.

AN AGENCY OF the federal government, the Pension Benefit Guaranty Corporation, insures pension plans—also known as defined benefit plans. The agency has a list of people who have earned benefits but could not be found by their employers. To see if you're one of the lucky ones, go to: www.pbgc.gov.

Know What Your Company Reports to the SEC.

REGISTER WITH FREE EDGAR and enter the names of stocks or funds you already own or are following. When a company on your list files a report with the SEC, you'll get an e–mail notice from Edgar.

INFO: www.freeedgar.com

Take Notes.

KEEP A LOG OF phone calls with your broker, noting his name, phone number and the time of day. Jot down specifics regarding any orders you place. Make a copy of your notes and fax or send them to his office. This simple procedure will keep your trades accurate and your broker honest.

Go Wireless.

TO FIND THE RIGHT cell phone service, check with wireless dimension. It tracks over 1,000 calling plans in 25 metropolitan areas. The search is free: www.wirelessdimension.com.

Spend the Very Last Penny.

IN YOUR FLEXIBLE Spending Account. If you don't, any money left on December 31 goes directly to your employer even though you funded the account. Last minute money user–uppers: dental and eye exams, annual physical, new glasses or contact lenses, immunization shots.

Check Up on Your Online Broker.

TO FIND OUT WHO you can trust, 1) Verify that the firm is a member of the National Association of Securities Dealers (NASD), registered both with the SEC and also in the state where it's doing business with you. This information should be on the broker's web site. 2) Go to the National Association of Security Dealers' website to see if disciplinary action has been taken against the firm.

INFO: www.nasdr.com and click on "About Your Broker."

Know What You're Not Supposed to Know.

THERE'S MUCH THAT others withhold. Knowledge is power.

Forget "Buy Low" and "Sell High."

WALL STREET PUNDITS love to recommend this strategy, but the truth is you'll know if you bought low and sold high only after the fact. Instead, set goals and stick to them. My favorite: sell your original position when your stock doubles in price.

Save Junk For the End.

INVEST IN JUNK BONDS only after you've invested in large–cap stocks, Treasuries, high quality corporate bonds, bank CDs and a money market fund. Junk bonds have higher yields, but come with high risk.

Retire, But Don't Retire Your IRA.

IF YOU STOP WORKING and no longer have earned income, but your spouse still has a job, together you can put $4,000 into a Roth IRA.

Get Your Social Security Status.

COMPLETE THE ONLINE questionnaire, "Request a Personal Earnings and Benefit Estimate Statement," and shortly, you'll receive an estimate of how much your monthly Social Security check might be. You'll also learn when you're eligible for full benefits, what happens if you retire early and more.

INFO: www.ssa.gov

No Amount Is Too Small to Save...

IF YOU SAVE $1 per day in a shoebox, at the end of 30 years you will have $10,950. Pretty thrifty.

— ¢ —

but...Save It in the Right Place.

PUT THAT SAME AMOUNT in an account earning 8% a year, at the end of 30 years, you'll have $45,009. (For those of you still counting on your fingers, that's a difference of $34,059!)

Don't Forget How Old You Are...

IT USED TO BE that if you waited until age 65, you could collect full Social Security benefits. No longer. The age is gradually being increased from 65 to 67, based on a sliding scale. Anyone 61 or younger now must wait at least an extra two months past 65, to a maximum of two years before collecting.

...and if You're 62

YOU CAN STILL TAKE Social Security benefits starting at 62 but if you do, your benefits will be reduced by as much as 30%. And that reduction is permanent. No going back.

Go for the Green.

HERE'S A NEW WAY to find socially conscious mutual funds—those that screen businesses involved in tobacco, liquor, gambling, weapons, nuclear power, excessive logging and similar companies. The Social Investment Forum gives comparative total returns and has the names of financial planners and brokers who specialize in this type of investing.

INFO: www.socialinvest.org

Save for College With Your State.

TAX–DEFERRED PLANS, sponsored by states and run by money–management firms, are catching on across the country. This type of account grows tax–free until the money is withdrawn to cover college costs; then, withdrawals are taxed at the child's lower rate.

INFO: College Savings, (877) 277–6496 or: www.collegesavings.org (This organization also has details on prepaid tuition plans.)

Learn to Thread a Needle.

THE LOST ART OF mending enables you to buy, repair and wear wonderful clothes from upscale thrift shops. In fact, finding someone who can mend is so rare you might make a fortune mending for others. As Henny Youngman said, "It's easy to tell when you've got a bargain. It doesn't fit." Learn to mend and it will fit.

Buy Insider Funds—Those Other Fund Managers Know and Like.

THIS IS LIKE GOING to the doctor the director of the hospital goes to. Most fund families offer a "fund of funds," which invests in other funds rather than in individual stocks or bonds.

Rethink Your Savings for Age 85, Not 65.

THE LIKELIHOOD THAT you'll live a long life is excellent. That means investing in growth stocks, not just income securities, long after you turn 65.

Don't Confuse Salary Reduction With Paycheck Reduction.

IF YOU'RE NOT participating in your 401(k) plan because you don't want your paycheck reduced, think again. A 401(k) is a salary reduction plan, not a paycheck reduction plan. Money that goes into a 401(k) comes from pre–tax dollars, not after–tax income. You are always ahead of the game.

And on the Seventh Day...

SHARES YOU OWN IN a DRIP (Dividend Reinvestment Plan) are often sold by the company only on designated days or weeks during the month. That means you can never be certain of the price you will get. If you can't live with this, ask if you can transfer your shares to a discount broker to control when, and at what price, they are sold.

Cut Through IRS Red Tape.

TURN TO A DISTRICT Taxpayer Advocate when tax payments were incorrectly posted, when you receive an IRS notice that's incomprehensible, when the IRS tries to levy your bank account even though you've paid your taxes, and for similar troubles.

INFO: Call: (800) 829–1040 or: www.irs.us.treas.gov

— ¢ —

Join a Healthy Chain Gang.

MANY HEALTH CLUBS go bankrupt, leaving you out in the cold. To protect against this, join a chain, starting with a monthly membership to see if you like it. (Nearly 45% of the people who join clubs drop out within six months.) Read the small print and make sure you have an escape clause in case you move, become ill or disabled.

Talk to Your Landlord Before Signing a Lease.

MAKE CERTAIN IT includes two clauses: 1) A transfer clause stating that if you're transferred by your employer more than 60 miles away the lease will end without a penalty. 2) A humanitarian clause that lets you out of your lease because of serious health problems.

Open an Education IRA for Each & Every Child.

YOU (OR ANYONE ELSE) can sock away $500 per year per child under age 18. The money grows tax–free and withdrawals are tax–free if used to cover college tuition, books, fees, supplies. **INFO:** www.educationira.com

Join a Credit Union.

YOU MAY THINK you don't qualify, but you never know. It's worth a try because their checking, savings and loan rates almost always beat those offered by banks.

INFO: To find out if you qualify for membership, call the Credit Union National Association: (800) 358–5710

The Perils of Forgiveness.

IF YOU'VE SIGNED UP FOR a debt–reduction plan and a creditor forgives a portion of your outstanding balance, don't toss out the documents. Some creditors must notify the IRS if they forgive at least $600 in debt, reporting it on Form 1099 that's sent to you. Then, you must report this as income and pay taxes on it. Yuck!

Go from B to B to A to A.

CORPORATE BONDS RATED BBB or higher are considered investment grade. Bonds ranked below this are considered "junk," or high-yield. If you're conservative, stick with 'A'-rated issues; if you have tolerance for risk, ask your broker to recommend junk bonds, but only those he would have in his portfolio.

Don't Be a Student Loan Deadbeat.

THE U.S. DEPT. OF Education, under a new law, is going after loans dating to the 1970s. Delinquents taken to court can be charged for the government's legal fees; once the government has a judgment, it can seize bank accounts, wages, cars, tax refunds, etc. Pay up. Contact your lender if you're far behind, but never ignore a student loan.

...*and Deduct Student Loan Interest.*

THIS DEDUCTION is available on interest paid during the first 60 months. Check with your lender to see if you qualify.

– ¢ –

Buy on Bad News.

BUT ONLY IF YOU know the company's fundamentals and you're certain the bad news has created only a temporary price dip.

Moves to Make When Baby Makes Three.

GET A SOCIAL SECURITY number for your newborn so you can claim him as a dependent on your tax return and open a savings account to hold all those gifts of stocks, bonds and cash. And, immediately enroll the baby in your health plan...some require that you do so within 30 days of birth.

Track the Dollar...

WHEN THE DOLLAR declines against foreign currencies, it makes imported goods more expensive, so think twice about major foreign–made purchases.

...and Lighten Up on U.S. Holdings.

A WEAK DOLLAR LEADS to the sale of U.S. stocks and bonds by foreign investors for better returns elsewhere. You may want to do the same.

Learn More About U.S. vs. Overseas...

GET THIS FREE BOOKLET: "Currency: Making Sense of Exchange Rates." For a copy, call: (800) 525–2440.

— ¢ —

Pigs Get Fat. Hogs Get Slaughtered.

TRANSLATION: MAKE money on your investments, but get too greedy and profits will turn into losses.

Turn Stormy Weather into a Profit.

DISASTERS—SUCH AS hurricanes, tornadoes and floods—boost consumer purchase of plywood, glass and other construction materials. Invest in lumber futures on news of a serious storm. And retailers, such as Home Depot, are often a wise investment before hurricane season.

Invest with Your Kids.

MUTUAL FUNDS THAT invest in companies of interest to children tend to report impressive returns. Buy the funds for long–term holding or call and ask for their top ten holdings.

- USAA First Start Growth: (800) 382–8722
- Royce Giftshares: (800) 221–4268
- Stein Roe Young Investor: (800) 338–2550
- Monetta Children's Express: (800) monetta

Never Buy Stocks on Triple–Witching Day.

THIS QUARTERLY EVENT takes place on a Friday when three kinds of securities expire: stock and index options and index–futures contracts. It leads to large buy and sell orders and erratic bouncing of prices. Change positions on Thursday or Monday.

To Roth or Not to Roth.

TO CONFRONT THE confusion about whether you should have a traditional or a Roth IRA, use the Roth IRA Analyzer at: (800) 368–1470 or: www.strongfunds.com

Boost the Gains in Your IRA.

SELL COVERED CALLS. This is the only option trade allowed in an IRA.

— ¢ —

Better to Ask Twice Than Go Wrong Once.

ADHERE TO THIS GERMAN proverb in all aspects of your finances. Ask for two analysts' opinions on a stock, two independent ratings on an insurance company, two bank CD yields and so on.

Don't Forget How Old Your Child Is.

IF HE OR SHE HAS unearned income (from investments and savings), the first $700 is tax free. The second $700 is taxed at 15%, the lowest bracket for federal income tax. After that, if your child is under age 14, any additional unearned income is taxed at your rate. But, the good news is that when your child turns 14, he pays the tax based on his tax rate, which unless he's a financial whiz, is most likely lower than yours.

Get Your Medical Records.

ASK YOUR DOCTOR to send you a copy of your file each year. Doctors are permitted to destroy their patients' records after a certain amount of time has gone by— how much time is determined by each state. For a medical history that may be public record, contact Medical Information Bureau, (617) 426–3660.

Investigate First. Invest Second.

BEFORE YOU INVEST money with someone you haven't worked with before, do a background check. These three organizations will help you find any negative information on both individuals and organizations offering investments to the public:

- NASD: (800) 289–9999 or: www.nasdr.com
- SEC: (800) 732–0330 or: www.sec.gov
- BBB: (703) 276–0100 or: www.bbb.com

Audit–Proof Your Return.

MORE WAYS TO COURT an audit: 1) Your itemized deductions represent an unusually large percentage of your taxable income; 2) You're self–employed and your gross receipts are over $100,000; 3) You take a home–office deduction; 4) You have large travel & entertainment expenses; 5) You claim large casualty–loss deductions.

Pay for College One Month at a Time.

HAVING TROUBLE FORKING over a semester's tuition in one check? Academic Management Services' Interest–Free Monthly Payment Plan, available at 1,500 colleges, lets you make ten payments on an annual basis or five per semester. The enrollment fee runs about $50.

INFO: (800) 556–6684 or: www.amsweb.com

Look Up Your Deductibles.

DUE TO THE FINANCIAL devastation from Hurricane Andrew, insurers shifted the cost of storms to homeowners by imposing coverage caps and higher deductibles—as high as 10%. (That means on a $200,000 home, a 5% deductible would cover only $10,000 worth of damage.) Be prepared. Check your policy. Consider moving inland or to higher ground.

Invest in the Growing Job Market.

BUY STOCKS IN industries where demand for workers is on the rise. According to the bureau of labor statistics, they are: 1) Computer specialists, engineers and systems analysts; 2) Personal & home–care aides; 3) Physical therapy; 4) Medical assistants; 5) Desktop–publishing specialists.

Skip Occupations with Decreasing Need for Employees.

THEY ARE: sewing machine operators, farmers, bookkeepers, typists, secretaries (except legal & medical), servants, farm workers, office machine operators and welfare–eligibility workers and interviewers.

Dealer Financing Versus Rebate.

CAR FINANCING IS tricky business. With low, low monthly payments you could wind up paying more on a car than it's worth. To determine when a dealer's financing offer beats a rebate, consult The Credit Union National Association's website at: www.cuna.org.

Sell When Your Fund's Performance is Behind Its Peers.

COMPARE A FUND'S total return figures with very similar funds and not against an overall index. Compare balanced funds with balanced funds; international funds with international funds, aggressive growth with aggressive growth, etc. Then, keep or switch to a fund that is leading the pack.

Spotting Bogus Banks.

THERE ARE SO MANY online banking scams that the FDIC has a "Suspicious Internet Banking" section on its website, listing organizations that are operating without authorization. These phonies use look–alike, sound–alike words and names. Favorites: "First," "National," "Chase" and the name of a city: e.g., First Bank of "X." **$TIP:** If advertised rates appear too good to be true, check with the FDIC at: www.fdic.gov.

Bad Weather Rattles the U.S. Bond Market.

INSURANCE COMPANIES tend to sell bonds to raise cash in preparation for huge disasters. Ignore if you hold bonds long–term; sell upon news of stormy weather if you're a trader. Ditto on insurance stocks.

Count Up Absolutely Everything.

LIST BANK ACCOUNTS, gold and silver, pension plans, insurance policies, securities, business interests, notes receivable, annuities, real estate, cars, personal property. You'll be amazed at how much you own. Then determine how each item will be transferred to your heirs. The three most common ways: through your will, through a trust or by contract with named beneficiary. Review your choices with your attorney.

Cut Post–Holiday Debt.

THE AVERAGE AMERICAN takes six months in the new year to pay off holiday–related credit card bills. So, this year, organize your gift giving: except for the children, toss everyone else's name into a bowl and draw just one name per adult. And assign a dollar cap for everyone.

Vet Your Benefits.

IF YOU'RE A VETERAN, you may be entitled to any number of benefits—outpatient pharmacy services, education, home loans, life insurance, pensions, disability compensation, vocational rehab. To find out, call: (800) 827–1000 or: www.va.gov.

Don't Label Your Safe Deposit Keys.

IT'S TEMPTING TO PUT these keys in an envelope and label it with the box number and the name of the bank. Thieves will love you for doing so.

Turn Headlines into Profits.

LISTEN TO THE BUSINESS news at least once a day and read the financial pages of a major Sunday newspaper every weekend. Follow industry trends, interest rates, the consumer price index, new housing starts, the unemployment rate. Profits and losses in stocks, bonds, and real estate never occur in a vacuum.

Get with the Home–Improvement Plan...

IF YOU LIKE YOUR HOUSE, stay put. Moving often runs as high as 10% of your selling price. Long term, you may recoup fixer upper costs if you do sell. Here's what Remodeling Magazine says the average homeowner gets back: Minor kitchen remake: 94%; New bath: 89%; New family room: 84%; Master suite: 82%; Deck: 70%; Home office: 64%.

...and Get the Right Loan.

FANNIE MAE'S NEW Homestyle Remodeler, for people with excellent credit who need cash, lets you borrow up to $50,000. FHA's Title 1 loan offers up to $25,000. Many utility companies have energy saving loans for up to $20,000—provided you upgrade your heating and/or air conditioning system.

...But Never Use Your Credit Card to Pay for Fixing Up.

INTEREST RATES ARE too high and interest is not tax deductible. Better bet: a home–equity loan or refinancing your mortgage.

Forget About the Drapes.

IF YOU GET A GOOD offer on your house, don't reject it just because the buyer wants you to toss in the washer/dryer, drapes and other items. Chances are your next house will already have a washer/dryer and the drapes won't fit. Go for it.

Get in Touch with Edgar.

THE SEC's website has reports and financial statements on most publicly traded companies, including 10–Qs (quarterly reports), 10–Ks (an in–depth annual report), 8–Ks (updates and financial changes) and schedule 14As (proxy statements). **NOTE:** Companies with fewer than 500 investors and less than $10 million in net assets are not required to file annual or quarterly reports.

INFO: www.sec.gov/edgarhp.htm

Think Twice Before Borrowing from Your 401(k)

MOST LET YOU borrow and then repay the loan, with interest, into your own account. However, you are paying taxes twice: the loan is repaid with after–tax money (that you've already paid taxes on) and you'll then pay taxes on it again when you withdraw money upon retirement.

Then, Think Thrice.

IF YOU CHANGE JOBS, you have just 90 days in which to come up with the cash to pay back your 401(k) loan. If you don't have it, you'll not only have to pay taxes, you'll also be hit with a 10% IRS penalty.

Don't Compare Apples and Oranges.

WHEN CONSIDERING two mutual funds or securities, make sure they're in the same category. It's misleading to compare a growth and income stock, a tax–free fund with a taxed fund.

Travel with a Notebook.

WRITE DOWN THE names of things you like: hotels, motels, restaurants, food, wine, stores, clothes, equipment, services. Call your broker to see if the manufacturer or firm is publicly traded. Buy the stock if the company's fundamentals are solid.

Pump Up Your 401(k) Plan.

ASK IF YOUR PLAN will allow after–tax contributions by taking more money from each paycheck. Although you won't get a tax deduction for this, it, like the rest of the money in the account, will grow on a tax-deferred basis.

Know How Big BIG is.

MUTUAL FUNDS THAT invest in stocks are divided into categories according to market capitalization of the stocks in their portfolios. The guidelines are:

- Micro-cap stocks: $100 million to $250 million
- Small-cap stocks: $250 million to $500 million
- Mid-cap stocks: $500 million to $5 billion
- Large-cap stocks: $5 billion and above

A Dividend is a Dividend is a Dividend.

ANY DIVIDENDS YOU receive from stocks are taxable—even those automatically reinvested in additional shares. Dividends as well as interest income are taxed as ordinary income—at the same rate as your paycheck.

INFO: Read "Investment Income and Expenses," free from the IRS: (800) TAX–FORM or www.irs.gov.

Skip Your Broker.

MORE AND MORE companies are selling shares directly to investors. Most charge a small fee and offer dividend reinvestment plans. Buy shares only if you would invest in the company if it only sold shares through a broker.

INFO: Netstock Direct at: www.netstockdirect.com

If Your Broker "Done You Wrong."

THE SEC'S NEW DIVISION, "Investor Assistance & Complaints," is designed to help you resolve mistakes and wrongdoings by a broker. You can e–mail them at: help@sec.gov or write to: Office of Investor Assistance & Complaints, SEC, 450 Fifth Avenue, NW, Washington, DC 20549.

INFO: For material on how to handle such matters on your own: www.sec.gov

Don't Just Say Yes; Instead, Negotiate College Loans.

ALTHOUGH THE government sets the interest rate on Stafford loans, local lenders may offer special deals. Ask if you can get a lower rate by making payments through an automatic debit plan or if you pay on time for more than a year. Read through the college's list of preferred lenders and then shop around on your own.

Invest Defensively, Not Willy–Nilly.

THAT MEANS BEING properly diversified to minimize risk and enhance profits. Own both stocks and bonds. Own both growth and value stocks. Own both large and small cap stocks. Own both U.S. and foreign stocks. Own both preferred and common stocks. Own both corporate and municipal bonds. Own both high–yield and investment–grade bonds. And, always own plenty of cash.

Know What Your Lender Knows About Mortgage Costs.

GET A COPY OF the HUD 1 form which lists all the legally allowed charges a borrower may be asked to pay at the closing. It will empower you to spot and challenge excessive fees.

INFO: hud.gov.us

Always Say "Yes" to Free Money.

IF YOUR EMPLOYER matches your 401(k) contribution, fund your plan to the max so that your boss will kick in the max as well. Contribute less and you're turning your back on extra cash.

— ¢ —

Go for Growth.

BUT CONSISTENT growth. A company that grows at 15% year after year is a better investment than one that grows 100% this year, 30% the next year and zippo the third year.

Pay Extra.

IF YOU PAY AN extra $100 a month on a $100,000, 30–year 8% mortgage, you'll pay off your loan in 20 years and save more than $60,000 in interest. **CAUTION:** Check with your lender first to see if you'll be hit with a pre–payment penalty.

Invest, Don't Trade.

IF YOU TRADE continually you'll not only run up commissions but you'll also trigger a taxable gain each time you make a profit. Think before you act. Better yet, think long term.

Make a Date with Your Stocks.

THE DAY YOU BUY a stock, set a sell price and a date when you expect it to reach that price. When the stock hits the target price, keep it if you're willing to buy more; sell if you're not.

Leave Home Without It.

IF YOU'RE HAVING credit card problems and can't resist running up debt, leave your cards at home, preferably in the freezer. Instead, carry cash and bank checks to cover everyday purchases and travelers' checks for emergencies.

Sometimes It Pays to Tell All.

TO REDUCE THE likelihood of an IRS audit, when you take an unusually large tax deduction, include a short, typewritten explanation with your 1040. Attach copies (not originals) of all documents that support your deduction.

Retire Your Mortgage Before You Do.

OBVIOUSLY. Often the most obvious is what we overlook.

Order a Mutual Fund Prospectus for Free.

THE LIPPER MUTUAL Fund Club has a prospectus for 500 funds. Select by fund family or your investment objective.

INFO: www.fundclub.com

Track Mutual Funds' Cash Positions.

WHEN CASH HOLDINGS are on the rise, it means fund managers are feeling cautious about the stock market. Time to lighten up and take some profits. **$TIP:** "Morningstar Mutual Funds," a research service covering 1,500 funds, gives this data. Call: (800) 876–5005 or check your Library or broker's office for copies.

Enjoy Getting Older.

WHEN YOU TURN 50, you can join AARP and get discounts on drugs, airfares, hotels, cruises, and car rentals. At 55, you can take penalty–free withdrawals from some company retirement plans upon leaving. At 59½, you can withdraw money from your traditional IRA without being penalized. At 60, if you're a widow or divorced, you can start collecting Social Security benefits. At 62, non–widows and widowers can start collecting Social Security benefits. At 65 to 67 you can start collecting full

Social Security benefits, depending upon when you were born. At 70, earned income no longer reduces Social Security benefits. At 70½—though minimum distributions must start from most retirement plans—if you're still working, you can continue to put money in your Roth IRA.

— ¢ —

Home State Loyalty Pays Off.

INVEST IN MUNICIPAL bonds issued by your state and you'll get a double tax break—the interest earned will be free from both state and federal income taxes.

Get Four Legal Documents in Order Now.

EVERYONE NEEDS: a will specifying how your estate will be divided and who will take care of minor children; a durable power–of–attorney authorizing a trusted person to make financial decisions on your behalf if you become incapacitated; a living–will giving details about whether you want life–prolonging medical care if you are terminally ill or unable to communicate; a health care power–of–attorney that authorizes someone to make all your health decisions, should you be unable to do so.

Pick Your Bank Carefully.

TO REGAIN CUSTOMERS, more banks are guaranteeing rates as high as the average money market fund; some are paying $\frac{1}{2}$ percent more. **$TIP:** For highest yields: www.ibcdata.com.

Slam–Dunk Deductions for Job–Hunting.

YOU CAN DEDUCT many expenses involved in looking for work, even if you don't land the job. But the work has to be in the same field as your current job. Deductions include: phone calls, resumé, postage, travel, and outplacement agency fees.

Mum's the Word When You're in an Automobile Showroom.

NEVER TELL THE salesperson you're interested in a particular model. He's likely to then load up the car with costly options you don't need. And, ditto on options. Don't tell the dealer what extras you want; let him throw those in for free to close the deal.

But Mum's Not Always the Word.

IF A CAR YOU WANT has options you don't want, negotiate tough to reduce the price. The markup on options ranges from 100% to 1,000% so don't be shy.

Control Risk. Don't Let It Control You.

AVOID TAKING LARGE positions in hot sectors of the stock market. It's impossible, even for the experts, to continually determine which industries will shine and which will ones will fade.

Head Up North.

SAVE THOUSANDS on college tuition by attending a Canadian college. Most are heavily subsidized by Canadian taxpayers, and the U.S. dollar stretches farther across the border.

– ¢ –

Never Automatically Roll Over a Maturing CD into a New One.

SHOP FOR RATES. Check newspapers and www.bankrate.com to find the nation's highest-yielding certificates.

Create a Road Warrior's "Must–Read" File.

FILL IT WITH ARTICLES and clippings on stocks, the market and other material related to your financial well being. Take it with you, along with a notebook and pen, on trains, planes, buses and subways…fill in the time by learning.

Panic Before You Buy—Not After.

PICK STOCKS THAT you can hold comfortably through scary drops in the market.

Make a Long–Term Decision Before Turning 70.

THAT'S WHEN PREMIUMS on long–term care insurance rise dramatically. Coverage runs about $1,800 a year for 55–year–olds and as much as $4,000 a year for 70–year–olds, provided they qualify.

Don't Stay Put. Get a Move on.

MONEY WITHDRAWN FROM 401(k) plans, IRAs and company pension plans is taxed according to where you live when you receive the checks. If you live in a state with a high income tax, such as California, Minnesota or New York, then move to one with little or no income tax, such as Texas, Nevada or Florida, you'll save money on state income tax. **CAUTION:** Find out how long it takes to establish residency (it may be a year) and what happens if you own real estate in two states.

Speak Up If You're an Innocent Spouse.

IF YOU WERE UNAWARE that your spouse took money set aside for taxes and used it for other purposes, the IRS can now grant you relief.

INFO: For details on this and other rulings, read IRS Publication 971, "Innocent Spouse Relief." Get it by calling: (800) TAX–FORM or: www.irs.ustreas.gov.

Skip Right Over Expensive Mutual Funds.

ACCEPTABLE MAXIMUM expense ratios are: 1.88% for international funds; 1.45% for U.S. stock funds; 0.75% for taxable bond funds; 0.66% for index funds; 0.50% for municipal bond funds; 0.25% for money–market funds.

The Trend Is Your Friend.

THIS TRIED AND TRUE commodity traders' adage works well for everyone: when the price of corn goes up and oil goes down, sell oil and buy corn. Make a list of ten stocks and options you'd like to own. Then, sit back, wait for an up–trend and buy at once.

Pay Less for Yakkity–Yak.

IT'S EASY TO GO crazy trying to figure out which long distance service to use. Teleworth to the rescue. It offers free comparison rates from 500 companies, including AT&T, MCI and Sprint. The rates quoted are the same as if you went directly to the companies. **$TIP:** If you're moving, they'll help you get set up in your new location.

INFO: (888) 353–9676 or: www.wirelessdimension.com.

213

Never Buy a Light Bulb Retail.

IF YOU'RE REMODELING or fixing up your house, before heading to the local hardware store, get the catalog from Maintenance Warehouse, a division of Home Depot. A favorite with building superintendents and contractors, it lists thousands of in-stock items and shipping is free. Next-day delivery is often available for plumbing supplies, hardware, appliances, tools, paints, cupboards, flashlights. **INFO:** (800) 431-3000

Cold Blood Leads to Cold Cash.

BE UNEMOTIONAL and methodical when investing. Feelings have no place in the market. Pick the price at which you want to buy and stick to it. Do the same on the sell side.

Know the Strength of the Dollar.

WHEN THE DOLLAR falls against other currencies, institutional money tends to move to the euro, the pound, the yen. Lighten up on U.S. holdings and move into well researched foreign stocks—they're likely to rise in price.

Find Your Lost Mittens…and Money.

THOUSANDS OF dollars go unclaimed year after year—utility deposits, old savings accounts, tax refunds—and some of these dollars could belong to you.

INFO: Get in touch with the National Association of Unclaimed Property Administrators at: www.unclaimed.org for the phone numbers and Internet addresses for state offices that hold such funds.

Stay Within the Margins.

KNOW PRECISELY what will trigger a margin call. (With a margin account, you can borrow up to 50% of your total account to buy other securities. The broker loans you the rest.) When your account drops below 35%, your broker will demand that you deliver enough securities or cash to bring your collateral back up to the required amount. That's known as a margin call. You then have five business days to come up with the money.

Find Value and the Stars.

TWO PUBLICATIONS every investor, pro and amateur, needs to know about are: Value Line Investment Survey, which continually reports on 15,000 stocks, ranking them for both safety and timeliness. (800) 634-3583; and Morningstar, which does the same for mutual funds (800) 876-5005.

Pick Stocks Using the Company's Return–on–Equity.

YOU'LL FIND THIS figure, which measures management's ability to make money, in the annual report. It's calculated by dividing common share equity (net worth) into net income, after preferred stock dividends and taxes. Above 10% is acceptable, above 15% is desirous.

Review Your Estate Plan to Keep It in the Family.

FOR YEARS, THE amount excluded from estate taxes was $600,000, then $625,000. Now, it's $650,000. The exclusion will increase each year until 2006 when it reaches $1 million. Talk to your lawyer.

Be Independent.

IF YOU'RE FILING an insurance claim due to storm damage, talk first to an independent public adjuster who will help document your loss, draw up the papers and negotiate with your insurance company. (Ask what the fee is.) And, only use one who is a member of the National Association of Public Adjusters.
INFO: (703) 709–8254 or: www.napia.com.

Know Your Rights.

STOCK RIGHTS ARE a special type of option that let you buy common stock in the future. There's no commission and you get a 5% to 10% discount. About 80% of stocks bought with rights outperform the market the year after they're issued. Rights must be exercised within a short time—typically within weeks. So pay attention to your mail. **$TIP:** If you don't own the stock you can buy rights through your broker. They're listed in the financial pages with "rt" following the company's name.

Check the Employment Figures.

THE NUMBER OF people working is an indicator of the overall health of the economy. When the figure rises, consumer spending and the stock market tend to follow suit.

Never Confuse a Bull Market With Being Smart.

IT'S EASY TO MAKE money when stocks are on a tear. Don't get carried away with success. Take profits. Keep diversified. Look for new opportunities.

Just Say "No."

IT's UP TO YOU to resist con–artists. They're skilled, quick, have answers to everything and know more about you than you do about them. If you have a mailbox, telephone or e–mail, you're a potential victim. For help in ridding them, read "Avoiding Phone Fraud" from the National Fraud Information Center, (800) 876–7060 or www.fraud.org; "Investment Swindles: How They Work & How to Avoid Them" from the Consumer Information Center: (800) 878–3256 or www.pueblo.gsa.gov.

Never Tell All.

SKIP QUESTIONS THAT are too personal when filing out information on the Internet. The Federal Trade Commission has excellent advice about what to tell, what not to tell and how to protect your privacy on the Web.

INFO: Consumer Protection: www.ftc.gov/ftc/consumer.htm

Speak Up: Ask for Stock Options.

IF YOU'RE OFFERED stock options by your company, take them. Best bet: "incentive options," because: 1) You only have to hold this type of option for six months before selling; 2) Generally you won't owe tax when you exercise incentive options; 3) Your gain will be taxed at the lower long-term rate of 20%. (With "nonqualified options," you'll owe ordinary income tax on the difference between the option price and the fair market value on the day you sell.)

Never Buy a Penny Stock.

To PROTECT INDIVIDUAL investors from high–pressure or unknown sales people, the SEC has a "cold call" rule: you must sign a "suitability agreement" and a purchase agreement when you buy a stock listed in the "pink sheets." The pink sheets cover thousands of stocks that do not trade on an exchange or on Nasdaq.

Better to Know Now Rather Than 18 Years from Now.

TO FIND OUT how much a year of college will cost when your child is ready to head for the halls of ivy, use the College Cost Projector. Download it online: www.finaid.org/finaid/calculators/cost-projector.html.

Hold on Tight.

To YOUR STOCKS, that is—for at least twelve months. Then, when you sell, your profits will be taxed at the lower capital gains rate—20%. Sell before a year is up and your profits will be taxed at your regular tax rate, which could be a whopping 39.6%.

Know Your Letters.

UNLESS YOU KNOW more about a company, avoid stocks with the letters "vj" next to their listing in the paper. That means the company is in bankruptcy, receivership or is being reorganized.

Use the 30–Year Treasury as a Market Indicator.

WHEN BOND PRICES rise, stocks decline as investors move into higher–yielding Treasuries, CDs and money market funds.

Know Even More Letters.

SECURITIES LISTED on Nasdaq are identified by symbols. A fifth letter signals something unusual: C: exempt from Nasdaq listing for a limited time; D: new issue of an existing stock; E: behind in required filing with the SEC; F: foreign company; Q: currently in bankruptcy proceedings

"You Always Pass Failure on Your Way to Success."

MICKEY ROONEY had it right—learn from your financial mistakes. Figure out why they happened and take a different path the next time round. If you bought a stock because of a tip from a golfing buddy, don't talk finances the next time you play a round of 18. Evaluate your mistakes carefully and endeavor not to repeat them.

Lighten Up on Insurance.

IF YOUR CHILDREN are grown, your 401(k) and other retirement plans are funded to the max and you've paid off your mortgage, you may not need life insurance. Ask the Consumer Federation of America to run a computerized analysis of your policy and recommend whether or not you should keep it. **INFO:** (202) 387–6121.

Clip Store Coupons Online.

VALPAK, THE company that produces those packages of store coupons that come in the mail, now has them online. Search by zip code and then by categories (household items, restaurants, groceries, transportation) or by the name of the business.
INFO: www.valpak.com.

Photocopy Your Savings Bonds.

KEEP THE ORIGINAL bonds and the copies in separate but safe places. If your bonds are lost, stolen or destroyed, get Form PD 1048 from your bank. Fill it out and send with the photocopies to: Bureau of the Public Debt, Savings Bond Division, 200 Third Street, Parkersburg, West Virginia 26106–1328.

Home–Equity Loan Approval in 50 Seconds in 50 States.

GET THE GO–AHEAD for a home–equity loan in less than a minute, 24 hours a day with Bank One (you do not need to be a customer). **$TIP:** Use this type of loan for serious reasons, such as college, and not just to bike and barge around France.

— ¢ —

Just Say No to Bank Fees.

TRANSACTION FEES add up quickly. But there are 300 credit unions and more than 120 banks that don't impose surcharges. For a no–surcharge ATM near you, contact The No–Surcharge Alliance at (888) 748–3266 or www.thecoop.org.

Pick a Top–Ten, Low–Cost College.

ACCORDING TO THE College Board, these schools, in the top 100 in terms of academics, are the least expensive for state residents: Appalachian State University • Florida International University • Georgia Institute of Technology • Indiana University of Pennsylvania• New College of the Univ. of South Florida• North Carolina State University • University of North Carolina, Chapel Hill • University of North Dakota • University of Wisconsin, Stevens Point • Virginia Polytechnic.

Spare Your Heirs.

FORTY STATES HAVE approved the Uniform Transfer on Death Security Registration Act (TOD). This enables you to pass stocks, bonds and mutual funds directly to heirs, skipping the delay and expense of probate. Because the law does not require brokerage firms and mutual funds to offer the TOD option, you'll have to ask.

Tidy Up.

IF YOU'RE A PACK rat, hate to file papers or are juggling lots of projects, hire a professional organizer to straighten things out, at home or at the office. To find the name of an accredited organizer in your area, call the National Association of Professional Organizers at: (512) 206–0151. List what you need done and then ask for a written estimate that includes the number of hours and the hourly rate.

Social Security Taxes
Just Got Easier to Pay.

IF YOUR BENEFITS are subject to income tax, you can now elect to have the tax withheld by the Social Security Administration. Then you won't have to come up with the cash to pay your tax on April 15th. You'll need Form W–4V.
INFO: IRS, (800) 829–3676 or www.irs.ustreas.gov.

Never Short a Stock on Wednesday.

OR ANY OTHER DAY, unless you understand shorting involves selling something you don't own. You're betting a particular stock will drop in price. If you're right, you profit. You borrow 100 shares of X Corp. from your broker, who then sells them at the market price; say, $40/share. Your margin account is credited with $4,000, less commission. If the stock drops to $20, you cover his sale by buying the same shares for a $2,000 profit. But if the stock goes up—say, to $60—you must buy it at \$60, or your broker will demand you cover the gap in your account. Knowing this, you may want to leave shorting to day–traders, professional pessimists or the shortsighted.

As they say on Wall Street:

> *"He who sells what isn't his'n*
> *Must buy it back or go to prison."*

ABOUT THE AUTHOR

Nancy Dunnan's many books on money and finance have sold nearly one million copies throughout the United States and Canada. Her down-to-earth guidance to American consumers is consistently prudent, and well-received by her readers.

Ms. Dunnan is a contributor to many consumer magazines, including Your Money, Parents, Readers Digest New Choices, and Bottom Line Tomorrow, and is heard on WNYC Public Radio in New York City and nationwide on Business News Network. She is on the Internet at www.women.com. She may be reached by e-mail at Dunnanbks@aol.com.